All in a Day

by Ann Rossi
illustrated by Jaime Smith

Phonics Skill: Consonant *Hh*/h/
High-Frequency Words: *are, that, do*

Do you see Nan and Nat?

Nat can hit the top of the bin.

Do you see Nat hit it?

Nan can hit the top of a tin can.

Nan can hit it.

Nat and Nan are hot, hot, hot!

They can fan, fan, fan.

Nat and Nan can nap, nap, nap.

They can see a man.

Nat and Nan are at the stand.

They can sip, sip, sip.

Look at that.

Nat and Nan are not hot.